T

How

I Go

WHEN

I Go

E

THIS IS HOW I GO WHEN I GO LIKE THIS

Weaving *and* Spinning *as* Metaphor

INTERWEAVE PRESS

Editor: Veronica Patterson
Design: Susan Wasinger
Production: Michael Signorella
Proofreader: Nancy Arndt

Interweave Press, Inc.
201 East Fourth Street
Loveland, Colorado 80537-5655
www.interweave.com

Printed in Canada by Friesens Corp.

Library of Congress Cataloging-in-Publication Data
Ligon, Linda C.
   This is how I go when I go like this : weaving and spinning as metaphor / Linda
Collier Ligon.
      p. cm.
   Includes index.
   ISBN I-93I499-76-4
   1. Hand weaving. 2. Ligon, Linda C. I. Title.
   TT848.L54 2004
   746.I'4—dc22

                                    2004006398

IO 9 8 7 6 5 4 3 2 I

CONTENTS

ACKNOWLEDGMENTS

There are many people to thank for this book: First and foremost, Linda Collier Ligon, who has taught many of us the value of living one's dreams; Marc McCoy Owens, who collected the essays from the archives and, in the early stages, helped get the book into production; Veronica Patterson, a former Interweave editor and published poet, who so thoughtfully read and captured the essence of Ligon's spirit in the essays she chose; Susan Wasinger, a talented designer and musician, who magically transformed Ligon's words into a design that feels just right; Michael Signorella, another superb designer, who assisted at the last minute with the book's production; Interweave's book publishing staff, who did everything to keep this book moving forward quietly until we were ready to announce it; and, of course, all the weavers and spinners who have shared their stories over the years and contributed to the richness of our lives.

INTRODUCTION

I'm looking at two *huipils*, blouse-like articles of Guatemalan clothing, noticing differences in the weaving. To an untrained eye, they look almost identical. On both, figures of birds, horses, women and men, woven in bright threads, dance around the bands of fabric. But if you turn the huipils inside out, you can clearly see differences in the weaving. One is woven with a vivid red thread as the background, intensifying and supporting the other colors. The other has bright threads poking through a natural background, the threads almost hidden.

These two huipils are from Nebaj, Guatemala, a small, hard-to-get-to village. One belongs to Linda Collier Ligon; one belongs to me. Neither of us knew the other owned a Nebaj huipil until I spotted hers hanging on her studio wall. And the uncanny connection goes further: The current editor of *Handwoven* magazine actually lived in Nebaj for a year, learning to weave and coming to understand the designs in the huipils and the traditions behind them. According to tradition, the huipil with the red background was used in ceremonies, and the other worn in daily life. It was no surprise to me that Ligon's was the ceremonial huipil and mine the day-to-day.

When did I meet Linda Collier Ligon for the first time? I truly can't remember—maybe at a weaver's conference twenty-odd years ago or at an Interweave Press event. However, as a reader of *Handwoven*, I felt that I had already met her. Through her essays in the magazine, I had come to know her thoughts about weaving, spinning, and life. I believe in the connectedness of life, and sensed that she and I were connected somehow. It wasn't until years later, that I had (and still have) the honor and privilege of working daily with her at Interweave Press.

This collection of essays from twenty-five years of *Handwoven* offers weavers and spinners a lens into her world. To those who don't practice these crafts, it offers a unique perspective on life. Weaving and spinning are her passions, but they don't contain her. She draws lessons from them that she shares through her writing. And like our huipils, my weaving stories and lessons connect to hers. As weavers, we both know about the warps that defeat us, the challenge of our stashes, and the community that we share.

She believes that once weavers commit to weaving, they're always weavers, even if they don't regularly weave. Ask her. She would say she was a weaver, but might not tell you how long it has been since she's woven. Weaving is in her bones. For her, weaving and spinning are processes more than means to an end—just as life is, just as Interweave Press is. What makes the Press successful is the ongoing creative energy, the passion for what we craft with our hands.

Her life is about making things up as you go and learning what to do, or not to do, the next time. And about realizing that her short attention span leaves her mind open to being snared by day-dreams that take her down unexpected paths, not knowing if a new idea will take hold and become a new venture. Today, sitting in a meeting, I listened in admiration as she pressed on passionately about weaving and spinning and the need to pass these crafts forward. You'll find the theme of "passing it on" in these essays. And perhaps the theme grows in importance at this stage of her life. Her weaving doesn't hold the same web that it used to, and it's time to change the weft.

Without Linda Collier Ligon's knowledge, but in her honor and in celebration of twenty-five years of *Handwoven* magazine (and the Press behind it), we've drawn together these essays.

Our huipils lie side by side, soon to return to our respective walls. But as I wrote this introduction, I needed to have them physically together, to be able to touch them. Only then could I see the woven colors and images, the two weavers who made them, the women who treasure them now, all of us—joining in this endeavor: *This Is How I Go When I Go Like This.*

— Marilyn Murphy, President, Interweave Press

STRIKE ANYWHERE: AN EDITOR'S NOTE

When I recall first reading through Linda Collier Ligon's *Handwoven* essays collected as candidates for this book, what comes to mind is a small box of Diamond matches that says "Strike Anywhere." Every essay gave off heat and light. That's my way of saying that any essay not selected for inclusion could have been—and someone else might have chosen it.

Of course I felt I was applying a principle or two, the main one being great delight. Some essays that aren't included had portions that served specific purposes (e.g., to introduce a new magazine or book Interweave Press was about to publish). A few others strongly depended on photographs that are no longer available. At least one gathered multiple reader responses to a question that a previous essay had posed.

After common threads began to emerge and the collection had a presumed length, the selected essays seemed to acquire zing from being with each other. Although the essays are presented chronologically, the table of contents (any table of contents!) is a guest list for a party. So what are the motifs and moves that I thought wove (or, as you'll read, "weaved") these essays together?

In addition to weaving and spinning, the motifs include hands (and thumbs), yarn, thread, tools, keeping (and hoarding), organizing, the author's attention span, change and continuity, honoring individuals, noticing fabric—all of these and life.

The moves include the quick turn of mind, the speculation, the digression, the quirky word play, the personal approach to grammar, the contrary view, the challenge, the gratitude, and the occasional admission.

You will find great riches in these essays—sparks, coals, flames, even fireworks! Each one ignites and "burns clean with minimal smoke."

Enjoy reading! Strike anywhere!

—Veronica Patterson

ANNIVERSARY

ESSAY

To write about weaving and spinning

as metaphors for life

should be easy, shouldn't it?

In which the author, Linda Ligon, unwittingly
(though wittily) introduces a selection
of her essays from the past twenty-five years...

Poets and dreamers have been comparing weaving and spinning to life for centuries, and I've been thinking about it myself for at least the past three decades. You've got your warp, the constants (though they have their ups and downs) . . . your weft, the material life deals you daily . . . your continuous thread . . . your knots and breaks, your raggedy edges, your rhythms and colors and patterns. Just like life!

Think of the burble of joy you've felt watching somebody's baby take its first staggering, drunken toddler steps. Or seeing the first tips of daffodils poke up in spring. Those little things that make you laugh inside and think how good it all is. I've often had that same feeling when a piece of cloth I'm weaving comes together with a color surprise or a bit of texture or pattern that works better than I ever dreamed it could. Or when the luscious colors of a variegated roving slip through my fingers at the wheel, making sunrise magic.

We use weaving and spinning as metaphors for life
    because weaving and spinning connect us to a rich past.
    because weaving and spinning connect our brains to our
        very own hands.
    because weaving and spinning connect us to each other.
For those of us lucky enough to have the skills, the tools, and the time, weaving and spinning give us meaning, balance, harmony,

peace, stimulation, community, friendship, joy—the fabric of our lives, literally and figuratively.

Motivational speakers often pose the question, "If you were on your deathbed, would you look back and be sorry you didn't spend more time at the office?" The right answer is, of course, no—you'd be sorry you didn't spend more time with the people you love, or doing the work that will make the world a better place.

I think maybe I'd be sorry I didn't weave and spin more, too. Because the more I do, the better everything else seems to fit together. The more I weave and spin, the more in touch I am with myself, the more meaning I find in my daily life. You know?

TOOLS

"When tools help a person

to achieve creative fulfillment,

maybe love of a sort

is not inappropriate.

Or at least gratitude."

"Chimp uses stick to fish for ants," the headline reads. "Otters use rocks as tools." These stories turn up in the newspapers all the time, and I know I should find them surprising, but I don't. I can relate! I have simple tools that are such extensions of my hands, that I use so unthinkingly, I can't imagine higher intelligence having much to do with it.

I have a 25-year-old kitchen fork that handles about 80% of my cooking chores. It's my whisk, flipper, poker, prong, baton—as necessary and versatile as my opposable thumb. And a short length of pine molding, polished smooth with use, that has burnished down acres of artwork here at the office better than all the fancy store-bought spring-loaded devices I've ever tried. And a cheap plastic reed hook, a freebie from some loom company, without which I could not sley my reed. These tools have all come to me by chance, not choice; did they happen to be just right, or had I adapted my ways of working to their shape and heft?

Some of my favorite tools, on the other hand, I've chosen very deliberately. A pair of really good sewing scissors; circular knitting needles with a nice, smooth join; a raddle I made myself of pine and finishing nails with just the right spacing. It's a pleasure to have these tools at hand, to know they'll do a good job without fuss or thought. I've often heard weavers say that they love their looms; the verb is carefully chosen, too—they mean love. Love that has grown from familiarity, trust, fidelity, and accommodation. When tools help a person to achieve creative fulfillment, maybe love of a sort is not inappropriate. Or at least gratitude.

As I scan my mind for other examples of tools that I use and care about, I realize that there's a personal character to many of them that's as important as what I use them for. I'm fortunate to know and like the people who built my looms and spinning wheel. So whenever I sit down to spin or weave, it's in a very real sense like sitting down with friends. I notice and appreciate their design and engineering decisions, I praise their good craftsmanship. There's a quality to my relationship with these tools that doesn't exist, you can be sure, with my refrigerator, or my iron. (Perhaps if I were acquainted with Gen. Electric, I would feel differently.) Some tools are gifts from friends, too—shuttles, drop spindles, other little hand tools. Using them always, always invokes the giver, and makes the process especially pleasurable.

Best of all, though, are the tools that have come from family. My grandmother's dainty ivory awl—I coveted it as a child, and even went so far as to work tedious little eyelet motifs in the corners of handkerchiefs just for an excuse to use it. My great-grandmother's thimble—so tiny it will only fit on my pinky finger, but I put it on sometimes as a talisman. A bead loom that my grandfather carved for my mother when she was a Campfire Girl in the nineteen-teens. It tickles me to think of my very proper little English grandfather, cast by fate into the rambunctious early Oklahoma oil fields, carving "Wo He Lo" on an Indian bead loom for his little girl. I used the loom quite a lot when I was a Campfire Girl myself back in the '50s, and got it out again recently for reasons that I can't explain. . . .

DAY'S BLANKET

"We came up with the idea

    for the blanket that very first year.

I would spin the warp,

    Day would spin the weft,

I would dress the loom,

    he would weave it off."

Some projects seem to take forever. This one started way back in 1984 when my nine-year-old son Day decided to get into the sheep business. It seemed easy enough. All three of our children have had chores from an early age—hauling water, pitching hay, milking goats, gathering eggs—and Day has always been glad to do his share. A couple of sheep would keep the pasture down, we thought, and I'd have all this lovely wool right in my own back yard.

We bought two white Corriedale ewes, Tish and Betty, from our friend Camille Cummings, who was known for her fine, soft, colored wools. They bore one adorable white ram lamb and two black ewes, respectively, and gave us two lovely white fleeces that spring. Sheepwise, it's been downhill from there.

We have learned that sheep raising is not a casual occupation: that progressive pneumonia and tetanus and worms and keds lurk where you least expect them; that two sheep can keep a pasture down, but two sheep plus three lambs will turn it into a mini-Sahara; that two or three or four fleeces a year are more than this working mama has any use for.

On the other hand, there have been rewards. Day has contributed meat to the family freezer and wool for family caps and sweaters. Pre-dawn chores, snow or shine, no excuses, have helped him grow up with more fortitude than most 13-year-olds I know. And we've all enjoyed some sweet moments in the spring watching his lambs boing around in the clover.

We came up with the idea for a blanket that very first year. I would spin the warp, Day would spin the weft, I would dress the loom, he would weave it off. It would be a real, bed-size blanket that he could even show off to his own kids someday.

Well, in the first place, it took me about six months to get around to scouring a fleece. Then we decided, for expedience, to send it off to be carded, but it took another couple of months to find a big box. Then the small company we sent it to had multiple problems that held the carding up for another six months or so. When we finally got the carded sliver back it was summer, and Day was at his fishing hole from dawn to dusk until school started again.

We started spinning that fall in a desultory sort of way, a bobbin here, a bobbin there. Then there were trumpet lessons, and orthodontist appointments, and scouts, and Christmas, and so on. We didn't have a plan or a deadline, so the project didn't move, and soon it was fishing weather again.

Finally this winter I realized that time was running out. I looked at my kid, and he was as tall as I was. What if he got his driving permit before we got the yarn spun? Would he still want to do a weaving project with his mom? Fat chance. I decided to take matters into my own hands and finish the spinning, and finish it fast.

Having found resolve, I've been amazed at how quickly the blanket has materialized. One or two 300-yard skeins most evenings, and the spinning was finished in a couple of weeks. I wove up a scarf-sized sample to trouble-shoot, finding that it would be a good idea to size the warp, and that it's absolutely important to use a coarse reed. The yarn is a moderately twisted singles at about 3600 yd/lb, sett at 14 e.p.i., threaded to a straight twill and treadled on opposites. The soft grays are black and white fleece carded together. The fabric fulled beautifully in hot water with quite a bit of agitation, and I brushed one side while it was still damp. It's soft as a cloud, but promises to wear well.

The blanket warp is on the loom now, all seven yards of it, and Day has started to weave. He's got a good touch, a good rhythm, nice edges. His own handspun has maybe a little more character than the rest, and that's okay. It's going to be a great blanket, finally.

DEFEAT

"That the yarn snapped

as I measured off the very first bout

was ominous."

I am confounded. Thwarted, conquered, vanquished, licked, lathered, clobbered. I am outdone. Whipped. And all by a cone of yarn.

I bought this cone of yarn several years ago, thinking what a neat challenge it would be to weave a really, really fine fabric. The yarn is a 62/1 unbleached linen, fragile and fine as frog hair. But it never occurred to me that I couldn't make it work. When the yarn purveyor wrote up the ticket, he said, smiling unctuously, "Let me sell you a bottle of this warp glue, too. You'll need it." That should have been a clue.

I thought about the yarn off and on for a long time, imagining the diaphanous fabric I would weave, imagining how patiently and perfectly I would make my warp, imagining how expertly I would flip my dainty shuttle through my perfect shed. It was one of those "someday" projects that was fun to think about, that I felt no compelling urge to get after. But when our administrative assistant, Karen Evanson, gave me a lovely linen handkerchief for Christmas, I thought, "I could do that, too." After all, I've been weaving three times longer than Karen, and her thread, a 100/2, was similar in weight, and she did such a lovely job. So I set myself the task of weaving a handkerchief out of my linen. A Bronson lace handkerchief with wide, mitered, plain-weave hems.

That the yarn snapped as I measured off the very first bout was ominous. But knowing that linen is stronger wet than dry, I steamed the whole cone thoroughly and proceeded with no further problems.

That my bifocals couldn't see the thread and the heddles simultaneously was a hindrance, but not much of one. I figured a way to hang my chin on the beater bar just the right number of inches away, and threaded all 900 ends with no mistakes.

That I literally wore out my favorite plastic reed hook while sleying the first time should have signaled that the task was not for the faint-hearted. But I sleyed away, and had to fix only a couple of crossed warps.

That nothing happened when I treadled the first shed, no threads lifted at all, well, that was discouraging. I began to suspect that I had my work cut out for me. The tiny hairs protruding from the unsized warps were grabbing each other so desperately that nothing would move. I found that I could pick the shed apart with my fingers, though, so I tried weaving a few picks that way. Oh, dear. Maybe my 80 e.p.i. sett was too close. I cut off and resleyed to 60.

This helped a little; when I treadled, a few threads would lift, while the others continued to huddle together in little matted clumps. I was keeping the warp quite damp to strengthen the fibers. Although this lent tensile strength, it also exacerbated the matting problem. Perhaps I should size the warp after all?

I cut off the mess I had made and tied on again. I lifted each shaft in turn, painted a weak solution of glue sizing on the raised threads, dried it with a hair dryer, went on to the next shaft. Indeed, the adjacent threads no longer grabbed each other. Now they simply snapped because they were so brittle. I repaired everything and misted the warp thoroughly to strengthen it, whereupon the glue, of course, glued it all together irrevocably.

So I have the remains of this cone of yarn. I will send it to the first taker on these conditions: that he or she weave something with it within a month, or send it back for the next foolhardy soul. That he or she provide me with a sample of whatever successful fabric is produced. That he or she share his or her secrets of success. Here are some hints that might or might not help: String heddles. Counterbalance action. Paraffin. I'll wait for the requests to pour in.

OLD STUFF

" 'Ten years ago, is this how you thought it would be?'

His question stopped me cold.

the fact is, I didn't think at all."

I keep stuff. Drawers of it. Boxes, notebooks, sacks, trunks. The habit runs in my family; not long ago my mother, after doing a bit of housecleaning, sent me my World War II ration book, good for a pair of baby shoes and a pound of beef. When Jane [Patrick] reminded me recently that this issue marks *Handwoven's* tenth anniversary, I got to rummaging around.

I found lists. An "empty" book full of ideas for a new magazine, compiled in the fall of 1978 on a plane en route to the first state conference of the Arizona Federation of Spinners and Weavers. My 1979 Daytimer with daily and weekly agendas of things to do as the new magazine took shape (including this cryptic and still useful memo: "Find missing items"). The guest list for the party we threw when the first *Handwoven* came off press, and at which I got embarrassingly tipsy.

I found letters. Wonderful letters from weavers who loved the new magazine, painful letters from weavers who thought it was a terrible idea. Our first inquiry about an error in the instructions: "Is the total thread count of the linen placemat warp supposed to be 210 instead of 21?" (Thanks, Joan Broome, for sticking with us all these years.)

I found old photographs. Photos of my four-year-old and his teddy bear wrapped in a handwoven afghan (he's 5'10" now and pats me on the head), photos of an irrepressible model in splendid handwoven raiment and a werewolf mask. Photos taken while tiptoeing through cow flops in Bill and Louise Green's pasture, climbing on rocks in a mountain park, trying to camouflage unfortunate threading errors with taste and discretion.

I found swatches, yarn bits, correspondence, notes of phone conversations, memories. Things have changed so much, and yet they're still the same. I still felt like a kid then in a lot of ways, wondering what I'd do when I grew up. Today I look in the mirror through my bifocals and note the laws of gravity and conservation of matter, and still wonder, at least a little. We were a staff of three then, working in one room, mostly on the floor. Today we are 23, surrounded by computers and copy machines and fancy phones, still working on the floor. We've put out 47 issues and have the process down cold, but we still worry about whether anyone will like them and fall all over ourselves when a beautiful piece of weaving comes through the door.

This morning, as Joe Coca and I worked on photographs for this issue of *Handwoven*, arranging and rearranging and laughing at all the old stuff I had hauled to his studio, he asked, "Ten years ago, is this how you thought it would be?" His question stopped me cold. The fact is, I didn't think at all. Just didn't think. *Handwoven* didn't come from special vision or clever planning. It came from hundreds of weavers contributing to it, from thousands of hours of staff effort, from hundreds of advertisers and tens of thousands of readers supporting it, every day, for ten years. Words are weak; thanks for all the stuff.

TIME MACHINE

"I felt I was winding my way

through throngs of ghosts . . .

ghosts of unknown spinners and weavers."

I put on my suit last month and went to New York to act like a publisher. In between appointments, I found a couple of free hours to go to the Metropolitan Museum to see a stunning exhibit of costumes from the Napoleonic era.

The show covered the years between about 1770 and 1825. There were hundreds of ensembles, for both men and women, including garments for which there aren't modern equivalents: redingotes, bodices, fichus, and such. An eighteenth-century woman's "afternoon" dress typically consisted of a voluminous underskirt; a bodice or blouse with long sleeves, full at the top and tapering down over her knuckles; a sleeveless, open-fronted over-garment; a shawl; long silk stockings; pointy shoes; and a reticule (very fancy little purse on a string; wonder what she kept in it? mad money? lipstick?). A gentleman's attire was equally elaborate: coat, waistcoat, shirt, lacy neckpiece, knee pants, stockings. Even the clothes worn daily by the "rabble" revolutionaries were more complex and decorative than what you'd find in my closet.

The show was organized chronologically, and the commentary pointed out how social change affected fashion in the volatile years of the Revolution and the Empire. In the years before 1789, the upper classes wore silks, cut velvets, laces, and hand-embroidered goods in showy patterns and colors, with much intricate detailing. Just after the Revolution, everything was red, white, and blue, and gentlemen gave up their pantaloons and long stockings for simpler long trousers. During the Empire, women donned slim, white bosom-baring gowns, looking like so many living caryatids. A brief but hilarious period of reaction among the young resulted in nine-teenth-century "punk," with outrageously colored, patterned, and shaped outfits, complete with little royal blue granny-style sunglasses. As Napoleon's delusions of grandeur grew, ladies and gentlemen of the court dressed in longer trains, finer silks, more elaborately gold-figured vests.

The show was amazing for the sheer volume of beautifully preserved garments. The curating (with the help of Diana Vreeland) was exceptional. The commentary included thorough and accurate fabric descriptions and historical notes. It was exemplary but for one large, unanswered question: Where did all this cloth come from?

As I wandered through hall after hall, craning my neck and throwing my back out to get close enough to see weave structure and fabric detail without being reprimanded by those tough New York guards, I felt I was winding my way through throngs of ghosts—ghosts of unknown spinners and weavers.

These clothes were created during the earliest days of the Industrial Revolution. Weaving was just beginning to move from the leasehold to the city; spinning was just evolving from the simple single-flyer wheel to the jenny or the cotton mule. The fabrics in this show were created by men and women working alone with hand tools or in rudimentary factories on equipment that demanded much hand control. And, dear reader, we're talking about flawless fabrics—wools as fine as muslin, cottons as sheer as chiffon, yards and yards of bobbin lace as delicate as nylon net, full-length silk coats embroidered all over by hand in tiny, precise patterns. We're talking about hundreds of lifetimes of work, just in this one exhibit.

After struggling with a 60 e.p.i. linen warp that just wouldn't work, and taking six months to get a 50 e.p.i. wool warp off my loom because I could weave only a few inches an hour, this show left me stumped. Why do I bother spinning and weaving? I don't begin to have the skills, the standards, or the commitment of these weavers of the past. If they had had the luxury of spinning and weaving for fun, as I do, what kinds of cloth would they have created? If I pride myself on simple 20 e.p.i. kitchen towels such as the ones I'm working on now, what did my weaving forebears feel when they handed over 30 yards of perfect 100 e.p.i. dimity (with handspun cotton warp!) to a court seamstress? What would I feel if I could equal their efforts? Why don't I bother to try? Why do I settle for slubs in my finer cotton handspun yarns, and kid myself that they add charm?

These are questions I asked myself as I walked down Fifth Avenue in the snow, past whooshing buses and honking automobiles, to my hotel with electronic locks and computerized billing systems and telephones in the john.

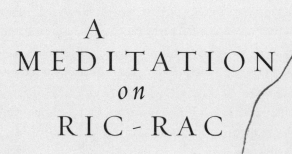

A MEDITATION *on* RIC-RAC

"*Perhaps if my mother hadn't laid me down*

for a nap on a chenille bedspread at age two,

I wouldn't have become a weaver."

Weavers have an eccentric trait in common: we notice fabric. We memorize the upholstery in airplanes, redesign the herringbone twill on the man in front of us in church, count the threads on our sleeve during boring meetings. How do we get to be so strange? My theory, based on personal introspection and a random sample of one, is that it starts in earliest childhood.

Perhaps if my mother hadn't laid me down for a nap on a chenille bedspread at age two, I wouldn't have become a weaver. I remember so vividly picking out the tufts and studying the resulting holes, and wondering. I remember running a finger along the puckered stripe in my seersucker sunsuit, and wondering. And watching an afternoon breeze blow the scrim curtain by my baby bed into folds so that it made moiré patterns, and wondering. Of course, there was an awful lot to wonder about in those days. Most of all, once I had figured out sort of how weaving worked, I wondered about ric-rac, and how the threads were made to turn corners every little way.

This was in the early forties. Fabric was scarce; my mother took apart clothes to make more clothes, unraveled sweaters to make more sweaters. Her scrap box was a major resource in our household, and it was always crammed full of trims saved from worn-out outfits, remnants bought on sale for 10 cents a yard, colorful feed sacks carefully unstitched, washed, and pressed. Like other frugal housewives, she worked with what was at hand. The necessity to "make do" informed taste and fashion to a large degree in those times.

The apron is a case in point. A prudent housewife wore one all day long. It saved her good clothes, saved on laundry. It did not, however, make a "fashion statement." It was designed from whatever jolly print was available and trimmed out with gay abandon: bias binding, tricky pockets, odd appliqués, cross-stitched cats or cups and saucers, or that mysterious ric-rac. Or all of the above.

I got to thinking about aprons recently when I found a set of old Lily "Practical Weaving" pamphlets in our library. One was a collection of handwoven aprons designed by a group called Twenty Weavers in the Washington, D.C., area. These aprons are much more stylish, tasteful, and intentional than the ones I remember from the neighborhood kitchens of my earliest years, but they prompted me to go to my yarn jumble (my equivalent of my mom's scrap box) and engage in a little nostalgia.

I wanted to use stuff that would never otherwise get used; hence the 20/2s cotton in a shade of pink that I detest. It's in the warp, alternating with ends of white. I wanted to weave a fabric that would prompt a very young child, sitting on a lap clad with said fabric, to trace the threads with her finger and wonder; hence the tick-weave color effect in the ground cloth and the one-block overshot pattern stripes. I wanted decorative elements selected with the same cheerful "why not?" attitude I remember from four decades ago; hence the random use of Mamie Eisenhower pink and green. There was something else I wanted, but I didn't find it among my scraps. A row of white ric-rac, to tack neatly along the bottom edge of the waistband.

TRUE
CONFESSIONS

"I will weave to satisfy my soul."

People often ask me if, with a full-time job and family, I have any time to weave. My stock answer over the years has been, "Of course! I weave almost every weekend!" For the past eight months or so, this knee-jerk response has not been true. I've had only two warps on the loom since last New Year's, and those two were no fun at all.

I've worried that I'm losing something that has been important to me for almost twenty years; I've worried that my life is getting out of control, or that I'm changing in ways I don't understand; I've walked past my empty loom and felt sad and guilty. But in a sheer panic about meeting the deadline for this issue, I've confronted some truths about myself as a weaver, and I think it's going to be okay.

The truths are these: I weave out of my feelings, not out of my head; and I really, really have no patience for sampling.

I'm finding both of these truths a little hard to swallow. I believe in careful planning and creative drafting. And how many times has this very magazine said "Sample, sample, sample"? I look at the work of some of our author/designers—Sharon Alderman, Carol Strickler, Kathryn Wertenberger, Jean Scorgie—and think, "That's what a weaver should be." That combination of inspiration, intellectual rigor, and disciplined craftsmanship. None of which apply to me as a weaver.

Please don't read this as self-flagellation or lack of self-esteem. I have plenty of confidence in my own taste and intelligence, and I truly like a lot of the stuff I've woven. But I'm finding that, for me, weaving comes from someplace inside that wants to operate intuitively, and when I try to force myself to work otherwise, I get blocked.

The blockage in recent months has come from trying to weave on assignment, or out of duty: a sampler for our upcoming eight-shaft pattern book, a piece for a theme issue that's not my theme, a gift for a person whose tastes are very different from mine, a self-imposed challenge to use up all my yarn before buying any more. My basement is littered with piles of yarn that I've pulled off the shelf, stared at, and wandered away from.

The breakthrough came last weekend. I had set myself the task, after procrastinating for three months, of weaving that darned eight-shaft sampler. It was an easy job: I had a threading, and needed only to sample for sett and play around with different tie-ups and treadlings. Half a day, and I could mark that one off my list. As I started winding my chaste off-white warp into bouts for the interesting modified point twill with deflected wefts that it was to become, something snapped. If you had been watching me, you would have seen only a flicker of my eyelids, maybe a little flinch. But inside, there was a tantrum going on. There was a really awful little Linda-Id in there stamping her foot and screaming "NO! I WON'T! YOU CAN'T MAKE ME!"

Well, I was surprised. It took me back to when my kids were little, and the helplessness I felt when they acted out that way. I never quite knew whether to hug them or send them to their rooms. In this case, I decided on hugs. I set that warp aside, walked over to my yarn shelves, and watched my hands pick up a big cone of dark brown wool singles. (I'm not exaggerating; I was really that detached.) I started measuring a warp, guessing at what I thought would be an adequate length for a simply-shaped jacket, conjuring up from memory what a proper sett might be for a moderately fulled fabric. As I rocked back and forth in front of my warping board, swooping the yarn from side to side around the pegs, I let my mind play on double-faced twill threadings and weft colors, and schemed on how, if my sett were too open, I could resley without jeopardizing the fabric width (so much for sampling). And I felt really at peace.

In retrospect, I believe that what had begun interfering with my weaving was a gradually evolving attempt to integrate it into the rest of my professional life: putting in my Daytimer when to plan the next project, and when to do the threading, keeping long-term lists of goals and tasks. If I were a professional weaver, that would make sense. But for me, weaving is a solace, a retreat from computers and calculators and book galleys and business reports. There's a difference between being professional and being serious.

Coming to understand this has meant accepting that I'll probably not ever be the kind of craftswoman that I most admire, and feeling that that's okay. It means that I will sometimes waste time and materials weaving off whole warps that will bomb. No doubt there will be times when I will be moved to quantify and sample and plan meticulously—I've done it before—but no longer will I make that a prerequisite to weaving. I will weave to satisfy my soul, and if the results are nice enough to give as gifts or show in public or publish in this magazine, that will be a bonus. I will weave to satisfy my soul.

BEGINNING WEAVING

"I remember the mystery

of a checkerboard pattern taking shape

as my strips wove over and under

(with a little help)."

Those of you who have followed my meandering thoughts in these pages over the years might recall that I come from a long line of savers, at least on my mother's side. This trait assumes different guises in each generation. My mother saves neat boxes (piles of them) full of neat packets of neatly labeled debris. I save my debris in undifferentiated heaps. My daughter keeps hers, old gum wrappers and all, in drawers. We hand our respective debris down, too. My mother periodically sends me select packets from her extensive collection; I give my daughter occasional gifts, such as a college graduation present of all the baby teeth that the tooth fairy had saved; and I'm sure she must be saving hers for her offspring, if not archeologists of the next millennium.

Going through a recent debris shipment from my mother, I found a real surprise in the packet labeled "1945." My very first weaving. I was three years old, and attending vacation Bible school at the Presbyterian church in Hobart, Oklahoma. Our dear teacher cut slits in sheets of construction paper and helped us toddlers weave in strips of a contrasting color. I remember doing this: I remember the low, scarred table and teeny chairs, I remember the chubby scissors that wouldn't cut, I remember the smell—and taste—of LePage's glue. I remember the mystery of a checkerboard pattern taking shape as my strips wove over and under (with a little help).

I frequently ask fellow weavers what led them to the craft. So often they cite a very early encounter with some form of weaving that comes back on them in later years. Finding my own first effort got me thinking about all the kinds of weaving I experienced before finally becoming a "real" weaver; I'm sure some of these nudged me along, though others were so frustrating it's a wonder I didn't develop fear of thread. Consider:

Paper weaving. Even though I regard my perky blue and white placemat with nostalgia today, I don't think it was a good introduction to the concept of "over-under." I remember that I didn't finish my piece in the allotted time. In fact, my teacher must have finished mine, and probably most of the other kids' as well. The project was too sophisticated for three-year-olds, and by the time a kid is five or six, dextrous enough to manage it, he or she probably won't be too thrilled with the resulting product. Maybe if the papers were glittery. . . .

Jersey loops. My brother and I received a hand-me-down jersey loop loom when I was about five, but not the loops to go with it. I wove a mat on it with my mother's scrap knitting worsted, but it made a shifty square that was useless as a hot pad or anything else. With a sturdy (not plastic) loom, proper cotton loops, and a patient adult to finish off the edges, jersey loop weaving is a marvelous craft for reasonably patient six-year-old children. And the resulting hot pads are truly useful. Now that my own children are grown, I bribe other people's wee ones to weave them for me.

Paper plate weaving. If you are responsible for craft activities for young children, beware of asking them to notch the edge of a paper plate, string a warp on it spoke-wise, and then fill in with scrap yarn weft. So many things can go wrong! If there's an even number of spokes instead of odd, it won't weave. If the plate's not extremely heavy, it will collapse. If a child doesn't have the patience of Job, or if the weft yarn isn't very, very fat, he'll never finish. And what if he does? What do you do with a paper plate covered with yarn?

Toy looms. You see these in toy catalogs for Politically Correct, non-sexist, gifted and talented children. They (the looms) have a little heddle bar that turns to make sheds, and little string heddles that can't be threaded a second time except by fairies. They come predressed with a cotton warp that can advance, theoretically. The box shows pictures of lovely shawls and smart placemats. I didn't have one of these as a child, but my two eldest did, and they were able to weave at least a couple of inches before it collapsed under the warp tension, or from being sat upon, whichever. Perhaps others have had more constructive experiences with these devices.

Plastic lanyards. Every Brownie or Bluebird or Cub weaves a four-strand-braid lanyard at some point. Nine is about the age when this usually happens, I think. The braiding is okay, but the truly exciting part as I remember it is making the square-woven portion just before the toggle hook. Over, under, over, under. Real tiny weaving!

Bead weaving. This may be an exclusively Camp Fire Girl activity, and it may have gone the way of Fords with tail fins, but it's my favorite recollection of childhood weaving, and a craft I enjoy to this day. All my children have given it a try, too, and have found it satisfactory. I think the charm, for kids ten years old or so, is that you can make rather intricate patterns, including initials and rude sayings.

Real loom weaving. I never saw a floor loom in action until I was in my early 20s, so I can only speculate about whether I would have been excited or bored. I do know that the times I carted a portable floor loom to my kids' elementary classes, warped and ready to go, virtually everybody got the eye-hand-foot thing immediately and stayed in from recess to weave off the many yards of warp I had provided. My reward has been the large teenagers who have come up to me on the street over the years and reminisced about this experience.

If we weave at all, and if we're ever around children, we're probably sowing seeds for the future of our craft whether we know it or not. I wonder what pivotal experiences you might have had as a child, or what effective ones you've provided for your own children or little friends. Won't you share them?

Passing it on

"Over and under/in and out./

That's what weaving's/all about."

I can't remember when I've written anything that resulted in more mail than my column of last January, "Beginning Weaving," sharing my earliest weaving memories. What wonderful, vivid, heartwarming letters describing your own childhood weavings, and telling of nurturing similar experiences with the children in your lives. Hearing from so many of you has given me the impetus to follow through on a ridiculous idea I had a while back.

Over and over again, your letters recalled that making a jersey loop hot pad was one of your earliest and best weaving experiences. The fundamental simplicity of process and the goodness and usefulness of the resulting product seem to have struck a common chord with children of a wide range of ages in generations past. The genuine enthusiasm with which these hard-wearing hot pads have been greeted by lucky recipients over the years—mothers, aunts, grandmas, and neighbors (as well as male counterparts who cook, of course)—must surely have reinforced the weaving experience in a positive way.

Wouldn't it be great to introduce thousands of new children to the joys of jersey loops? Children who might otherwise get the mistaken idea that fiber is stuff that grows on the manes of little pink plastic ponies, or that weaving is something you do in and out of space traffic on a video screen? Wouldn't it be excellent if all 35,000 *Handwoven* readers simultaneously taught 35,000 enthusiastic children how to weave a hot pad?

The plot thickens. What if those 35,000 children all sent their jersey loop hot pads in to the office of a certain weaving publishing company for a group photograph, and in due time received their hot pads back with a certificate of achievement? Something in me says that this would be nonsense, but something else says it would have some positive, if subtle, reverberations over time. Something also says it would be fun.

Except for a kid category in our "Teach a Friend to Weave" contest back in the early 1980s and a very occasional article, we've never really done much to recognize the weaving efforts of children in *Handwoven*. This "Great Jersey Loop Caper" I'm imagining would give children from four or so on up to the Age of Insolence and Condescension the opportunity to have a little fun with weaving and to get a special pat on the back for it. If you have time in your life to locate a loom and some loops, and to sit down for thirty minutes or so with one or more children of your choice, then please read on.

The Great Jersey Loop Caper

- Who can participate? Children of all ages, teachers of all ages. One teacher can teach multiple children; the teacher who teaches the most children will receive a lifetime subscription to *Handwoven* magazine.
- What does an entry consist of? One or more jersey loop hot pads woven by a child. It's okay if the teacher helps a little with those last tight rows, and with finishing off the edges. Each pad must have a label firmly attached with the name, age, and address of the child, and the name of the teacher.

Two 29-cent stamps per hot pad should be paper-clipped to the label if you want the hot pad returned.

- When is the deadline? Hallowe'en. The pads will be returned by early December so they will be available for Christmas giving. Each child will receive a special certificate of recognition. Send your hot pad (we suggest using a Jiffy mailer) to "Kids Weave," Interweave Press, 201 East Fourth Street, Loveland, Colorado 80537.

- Where do you get looms and loops? Plastic looms and nylon loops are available at most variety, discount, and craft stores. They're a little hard to work with, but reasonably satisfactory. The old-fashioned metal looms can be found at flea markets or ordered, along with good-quality cotton loops in pretty colors, from Hearthsong (call 1-800-533-4397 for a catalog). Maybe you could cut loops from the good parts of worn-out socks.

- You don't know how to make a jersey loop hot pad yourself? Send a self-addressed, stamped envelope to Jersey Loops, Interweave Press, 201 East Fourth Street, Loveland, Colorado 80537, for explicit instructions.

So unless you have better things to do, grab a kid, grab a loop loom, and do your job. Here's a little song, original, I might add, that you can sing as you weave:

Over, under
In and out,
That's what weaving's
All about.

Weave and weave
Until you're done.
Ain't weaving hot pads
Lots of fun?

ODDS *and* ENDS

"But to spin for hours and hours

and not have enough yarn

for even a simple knitted hat

is ridiculous."

I went to my basket of handspun yarn the other day to find material to knit a hat. I have quite a large basket of hand-spun and really didn't expect a hat's worth to be a problem. Here's what I found:

1 small skein red/purple variegated singles
1 skein brown/tan tweedy singles
1 gnarly skein of something blended with mohair
1 ball rainbow-dyed purple/teal/rust wool
1 small skein strange hairy unknown thing
1 small ball fine linen
2 skeins dark brown wool overdyed with red
2 small skeins light gray wool
. . . and so on.

In short, there was nothing that went together and not enough of any one sort for even a headband. In fact, there wasn't enough of anything to make anything.

I've often pondered the relative values of process and product, and tend to come down on the side of process. I spin and weave because I love to; what comes out of that activity is a bonus, or so I've always said. But to spin for hours and hours and hours and not have enough yarn for even a simple knitted hat is ridiculous.

Most of the problem is one of personality. I have a short attention span and become bored once the outcome of a project is clear. (How many of you love to plan, measure, wind, thread, sley, and weave . . . the first two inches? I thought so.) It occurred to me, as I surveyed my yarn basket with consternation, that I could have spent the same time spinning the same number of different kinds of things and ended up with a beautiful sweater, coat, afghan, or even pup tent if I had simply put a little planning time into what fibers in what colors I bought in the first place. A little more intention somewhere along the line could have made the difference between a veritable flea market and a useful store of yarn, without compromising my passion for variety.

This small but revealing incident has spawned a whole raft of resolutions:

1. I will not buy any more little bits of fiber (unless they're really wonderful).

2. I will finish spinning each bunch of fiber before I proceed to another bunch (unless I can't help myself).

3. I will rearrange all my yarns and fibers, currently organized by color because they look so lovely that way, by utility. No more fuzzy mohair in with dish-towel yarn (unless they look made for each other).

4. I will ruthlessly dispose of any yarn that I've had more than ten years and will surely never use (unless it has sentimental value).

That should just about do it. I handled my random wardrobe in much the same fashion years ago by having my colors "done" and never again buying anything that wasn't blue-green, brown, rust, or purple. Now I can get dressed in the dark. Applying the same sense of purpose and discipline to my craft will, perhaps, let me have my hat and spin it, too.

COMING OUT EVEN

"It's tempting . . . to fall back on the time-worn

metaphors that spinning has ever offered

for the patterns of our existence."

Have you ever tried spinning a space-dyed roving? Having a new hue come up every few yards and watching the colors blend into each other in between changes is so compelling that it's hard to stop. And for someone with an attention span as short as mine, the little "carrot" of a favorite color coming up every few minutes can be highly motivating.

Recently, I spun yarn from one of the multitude of dyed rovings available to handspinners today—a blessing for those of us disinclined to do much dyeing or other fiber prep. The palette was a curious combination of violet, eggplant, and warm brown with an unexpected element of a sort of acidic olive green. I would never have ventured the green myself, don't particularly like it as a color, but I'm glad someone was bold enough to put it in there.

The spinning occupied quite a few spring evenings. I had a lot on my mind, so just sat and let the colors flow. This has been a year of change. A dear friend passed away, and then my father. A treasured colleague chose to take another path, another moved away, another left to have a child. These are not tragedies; they are life. We all experience change and loss, and we move on. Not that it's easy; our minds want a lot of time to settle and adjust. It's tempting, in such circumstances, to fall back on the time-worn metaphors that spinning has ever offered for the patterns of our existence, and during my spring spinning, I did not resist. It was all there: the fiber, the thread, the rhythm, the continuity, the lumps, the breaks, the changing colors. No wonder so many of us find spinning so soul-satisfying.

What I didn't think much about as I spun was what would come later—the weaving. If you've ever woven with variegated yarns, you know that rude surprises often happen. The color sequence might be so regular that your cloth has tacky stripes or blobs where you were expecting a pleasantly random, tweedy effect. Or it might be so irregular that the whole thing looks like mud when you were hoping for a neat plaid. Furthermore, you can't really sample accurately, because without the full length and width of warp and weft, you won't see how the colors are going to behave. In very regularly variegated commercial yarns, you can measure the color segments and manipulate your warp according to a plan. The wool I was spinning was dyed in a repeating color rotation, but the color spacing was not uniform, and my spun yarn was far from uniform in diameter, as you can see, so the periodicity of the colors varies greatly.

Even so, I planned ahead to the extent that I spun the warp from the full thickness of the roving so that the color segments are several yards long. For the weft, I split the roving into quarters lengthwise in hopes that, with more frequent color changes, fat weftwise stripes won't develop.

My sample gave good sett and shrinkage information, but not a clue about pattern. In making the 5-yard warp which will ultimately become a jacket, I experimented with paddle-warping eight threads at a time versus a single thread, and found that it didn't make a lot of difference. There simply are going to be occasional spots where that assertive green piles up and calls attention to itself. The remedy will be to pull out the offending warp as necessary and replace it. Or decide to like it.

In general, weaving is a quantifiable, rational craft. All of its steps and elements can be planned, counted, analyzed, fixed in place, controlled. It will be interesting to weave a piece of fabric that has such a wild unknown as random color at work in it. I don't necessarily recommend going at things this way, but somehow, just now, it seems okay.

OLD THREAD

"There's nothing special

in this miscellaneous lot of stuff

except the stories."

Without meaning to, I've acquired a lot of old thread. First I inherited my great-grandmother's sewing basket, then I bought a bag of miscellaneous crochet cotton in an antique store, then an old friend sent me her mother's tatting detritus, then I found a box of fine looking wooden spool thread in a flea market. It adds up. There's nothing special in this miscellaneous lot of stuff—except the stories.

My great-grandmother moved from Tennessee to Indian Territory with her husband and nine children in 1896. I don't know much about her except that she was kindly-looking in photographs and surely long-suffering, given the wildness of my six great-uncles and the rigors of farm life in a new, raw country. Her sewing basket is a clutter of hooks and eyes and snaps, hem tape and elastic, papers of pins, needles, shirt buttons—the usual. In the bottom, though, under all the mending oddments, are spools of fine silk sewing thread in the most elegant range of colors imaginable. Bronze, copper, coral, cerise, pale shell pink—subtle, warm, sophisticated hues. And they've never been used.

Maybe she planned something fine for one of her three daughters, but time slipped away. Maybe she aspired to something special for herself—though she wears black in all the old photos. Or maybe she bought them just because they were pretty. Maybe she took them out from time to time and held them up to the light to admire their soft sheen. I do that myself sometimes. I like to imagine her sitting on the porch where the light was good on a fine afternoon with a stack of routine mending to deal with—all those work shirts and overalls—sneaking a look now and again at her lovely, lovely colors.

The bag of crochet cotton came from a dusty shop in a very small town in Oklahoma right on the boundary between the Osage and Cherokee nations. This little town has hardly changed since my mother was born there in 1910: everybody knows everybody; women are housewives and men keep their Stetsons on when they eat downtown. My "crochet lady," whoever she was, was classic in her tastes; all her thread is white, ivory, cream, or ecru. She had every size from gossamer lace thread to heavy bedspread cotton. And she sampled! Every ball of cotton has a fragment of work dangling off the loose end, and small bits of raveling pattern samples are tucked in the holes of the spools for safekeeping. There are bits of filet crochet, abandoned doily centers, two-inch lengths of lace edgings, a single cunning little treble-stitch daisy.

Maybe these were prototypes for full-sized dresser scarves and luncheon sets and tablecloths that actually got made, but I think not. I think this woman was an optimist with no staying power. I'll bet she changed her hairdo often and hated that hot prairie wind. I can imagine her finding a pretty, new pattern, buying a spool of thread, working enough to see what it might look like, and then feeling completely defeated by the prospect of repeating that same piece of work dozens if not hundreds of times more. I think she could have been my sister in another time.

My friend's mother, the tatter, was a different sort entirely from the crochet lady. Her balls of thread are as uniform and cheerful as a basket of Easter eggs: mint green, canary yellow, sky blue, baby pink (variegated with white, more often than not), all on neat 60-yard spools. This woman knew what she liked, and she did not mess around. Her tatting shuttle is purely functional, an unadorned aqua celluloid torpedo, built for speed.

Did she really scrub her kitchen to a shine, dust her parlor furniture, sweep the front steps, plump up all the pillows, and take a hot dish to a sick neighbor every day before sitting down to turn out yards of little tatted edgings with her neat, swift, capable hands? Or am I imagining things? The tools and materials seem to speak so clearly.

In contrast to the competence and good humor implied in the little basket of tatting cotton, the saddest story in my collection is my flea market find. Imagine a spool rack filled with the following: Three large spools of black cotton thread, five small ones. Four small spools of darkest navy cotton thread, one of slightly brighter navy. One spool of dark brown. One of darkest maroon. Four of a dull olive green. One of dark gray, two of medium gray. One small spool of gray buttonhole twist.

Was she a widow with an old-fashioned sense of propriety about her wardrobe? Or was she just gloomy? Each spool has only a few yards missing; she must have used them to sew on buttons and darn little problem spots, not to sew up anything new. Maybe she had an overbearing, boorish husband and all the thread went to mend his drab suits. But why did she keep buying new spools of the same colors? Maybe it was an excuse to go downtown. Maybe a nickel spool of black thread was her idea of a shopping spree. Maybe she had a post-Depression fear of running out.

I have one of those coffee mugs that says, "Whoever dies with the most yarn wins." I say, whoever dies with any yarn at all just might be setting herself up for rude speculation. I say we'd all better get busy weaving.

THIS IS HOW I GO
WHEN I GO LIKE
THIS

"My wrist learned from her hand;

it was that subtle and that direct,

and it made all the difference."

I try to keep up, I really do. I've listened to the rap music, scrutinized the grunge, tried to make sense of *My Cousin, My Gastroenterologist*. When one of my sons gave the other some "alternative" comic books for Christmas, I dutifully read one and struggled to find the humor in a beer-guzzling, foul-mouthed third grade dropout in a pointy hat whose conversation consists largely of "I hate you" and "Eat some paste."

It actually was pretty funny, in an existential way, and a line from one panel stuck in the back of my mind—a bit of nonsense waiting for a meaning: "This is how I go when I go like this." This loony mantra had me doing little shuffle-dances around the kitchen, striking slightly odd poses while waiting to cross the street at traffic lights, and engaging in various other regressive motor behaviors for several weeks (when no one was looking). And at some point I began to "get it."

Like when I tried to teach my daughter over the telephone how to make pie crust. The easy parts to tell, such as how much flour and how much shortening, are almost beside the point. The steps that make all the difference—when you've cut the ingredients together sufficiently, how much water to add depending on the relative humidity, how firmly to gather the dough together, how to do the feathery little strokes with the rolling pin—these do not yield easily to language. Your hands and eyes learn from the ingredients how they should feel, how they should look. Or else you learn while watching your mother, who will tell you in essence, "This is how you go when you go like this."

The gentleman who cuts my hair learned his craft in Europe as an apprentice, not in a beauty school, and the first three months of his study consisted of keeping his mouth shut and watching. Then he was given a pair of scissors and told to do a haircut, perfectly, "or else." You don't discuss your haircut with this fellow, and you don't always like the one you get, but you can be sure it is precisely crafted. His hands know the job, and they learned it from his eyes.

I worked at spinning cotton with a charkha off and on for years with unsatisfactory results. I had read all about the fiber and the amount of twist necessary to make a sound yarn, and I understood the mechanics of my little spindle wheel. But my yarn was consistently inconsistent, with soft spots and overtwisted kinks, until a great spinning teacher literally took hold of my wrist and gave it a little flip at the end of a draw while the twist ran into the yarn. She could not have told me in words how to do this. My wrist learned from her hand; it was that subtle and that direct, and it made all the difference.

Deborah Chandler (author of *Learning to Weave*) and I have been working together on a revised edition of her book to celebrate its tenth year in print. A major part of the work is the addition of a chapter on warping from back to front, and in trying to distill a general method to present, Deborah has talked with a lot of different weavers and watched them perform this basic task. The obvious steps are easy to quantify and write down—but not the small fleeting motions, the ones a weaver doesn't even know she's doing, that make the difference between a smooth, speedy process and a clumsy one, between a good warp and a troublesome one. So how do you convey those subtleties in print? It boils down to "This is how you go when you go like this."

Of course, much about spinning and weaving can be measured, recorded, and followed like a recipe: threading and treadling sequences, ends and picks per inch, grist, twists per inch, yards per pound. But those elements alone don't make great yarn or great cloth. It's the hand skills, the eye-hand response to the materials, the touch that set excellent handmade yarns and fabrics apart from machine-made ones. And learning those skills—when to stop fulling a handwoven fabric, how taut a closely set linen warp should feel when you pat it, how much resistance you exercise before letting a given spun fiber wind on the bobbin—are all very particular to the job at hand, and all highly self-referential.

I don't think the artist who created our obnoxious young character had any of this in mind when he wrote his catchy little conundrum. But it fits, don't you think?

KEEPERS

"When she dies, her instructions

were that the bulldozers should come

knock the house and all its contents down

and bury the lot."

You can organize your yarn by color, which can be very pretty, or by fiber, or by grist, or by what kind of thing you had planned to make out of it when you first purchased it, if you can remember. You can organize it by quantity (enough to make a blanket vs. enough to make a warp for a small towel). You can even sort according to how much weaving time might be required of any given lot and thus integrate your yarn management into a larger time management program, if you're so inclined. Or organize it by how each yarn unit is organized: put all the spools together, and all the cones, and perhaps hang all the skeins in artistic bundles.

You can store it on shelves (open or closed), in ice cream tubs or fancy wire bins, in handmade baskets or old plastic laundry baskets or fruit crates. You may not store it in various boxes neatly covered with wallpaper left over from your kitchen or with self-sticking shelf paper so they will all match; the time making the boxes presentable would be much better spent weaving, or at least thinking about weaving.

The little odd bits left over from actually making something can go in shoe boxes or plastic storage trays or egg cartons (if they're really little). Thrums are something else again because while their individual elements are little, they often add up to rather large wads. You can chain them if they're long, since they might sometime make a short warp for a little bitty loom that you might someday own, or put them in old transparent bread sacks or tidy Ziploc bags, or secure them with rubber bands and toss them casually into a thrums basket.

Maybe you could even organize your yarn chronologically according to when you bought it; this would lend itself to plans about using up the old stuff first. It would also be nostalgic and offer insights into personal and social history (such as that shade of green!).

If you don't have a single location to keep all your yarn in, but rather spread it around the house in a drawer or closet here, an under-the-bed storage container there, then by all means consider organizing it according to that which you really, really plan to use soon and that which will not be required in this lifetime. Or alternatively, by that which is very pretty and an inspiration to look at, and that which is ugly beyond any recollection of why you bought it in the first place (which very likely intersects with the chronological method).

All these suggestions are only the tip of the iceberg when it comes to storage. We will not talk about grease fleece, washed fleece, tops, rolags, punis, linters, mawatas, and especially-interesting dryer lint, for many of the yarn storage schemes apply to these items as well. But you must also deal with small tools, such as all the reed hooks which are not your favorite one, and the bobbins that flop or bind, as well as the bobbins that still have a very great deal of very fine yarn from a very-long-ago project left on them, which must be wound off if you're to use that bobbin again, and then what will you do with the yarn.

There are also workshop notes, planning notebooks, journals of your creative growth, clippings from old fashion magazines that show capes and suits that actually could be woven using yarn that you actually own, if you wanted to, and photographs from old calendars that have wonderful color sequences to be emulated (except that you'd have to buy more yarn, or take up dyeing). There are yarn samples that need to be categorized according to whether they are or are not obsolete and, if the latter, whether they are or are not useful for color inspiration or for keeping a young child happy on a rainy afternoon, if you happen to get a young child around and the television happens to blow up.

And what about the magazines?

I know a true story about a wise Osage Indian woman in northeastern Oklahoma, a wealthy widow whose very large home was simply packed with a great many interesting things (though they had nothing to do with weaving). When she died, her instructions were that the bulldozers should come knock the house and all its contents down and bury the lot. And it was done. Whether this has to do with taking it with you, or not taking it with you, or with creating a twentieth-century Indian burial mound to confound future archaeologists, is moot. It has merit.

New Key to Weavers

"Not that weavers are likely to be a danger

to anyone but themselves, but isn't it time

that we had a similar system for classifying ourselves?"

At Convergence in Minneapolis this past summer, I was struck by how much weavers are alike, and how much they are different. I was struck to a similar degree during a recent weekend at our family's little mountain cabin by how much mushrooms are alike, and how much they are different.

Weavers may work on big complicated looms, or no looms at all; they may weave with gossamer threads or industrial rope; they may create intricate, inscrutable structures or simple, bold plain-weaves. At a gathering such as Convergence, the types are fairly clear, at least during seminar sessions: all the flat–loom-controlled–multi-layer weavers are in one room, all the space-dyed-warp–plain weft weavers in another, and so forth. In everyday life, it's not always that easy to know who's who.

By the same token, mushrooms may be flat or domed, gray or red or brown, tubed or gilled, veiled or not, and so forth. They may have a long, hollow, deeply pitted or honeycombed cap (no veil, no ring) and be perfectly delicious, or have a long, hollow, deeply folded cap (no veil, no ring) and kill you, to name one confusing and extreme example.

In the case of mushrooms, fortunately, there are carefully worked out keys to identification and commonly understood names: few mycologists would mistake a *Morchella esculenta* (morel, good) with a *Gyromitra esculenta* (brain mushroom, bad). Not that weavers are likely to be a danger to anyone but themselves, but isn't it time that we had a similar system for classifying ourselves?

Much of the taxonomic classification of weavers—kingdom,

phylum, class, order, and family—is well established and beyond discussion. It's when you get down to genus and species that the system could use some improvement. Homo? You've got to be kidding. Ninety-five percent or more of handweavers are women. And sapiens, referring to knowing and reasoning, is very flattering, but knowing what? How to draft a network weave? How to keep tension on a backstrap loom?

And before you even consider those fine points, you have to distinguish weavers (those who put one long thread over and under and perpendicular to a bunch of short threads) from knitters and crocheters (those who loop one long thread together over and over again using 1) two straight sticks or 2) one hooked stick). It's a complicated business, this classification of things.

Think, for instance, of making the fundamental distinction among weavers whose warp threads do not show: is it because the warp threads are covered by weft (*Textrix tapestra*), or because the warp threads are still in the cupboard instead of on the loom (*T. procrastinata*)?

The challenge exceeds my memory of high school Latin and rudimentary understanding of taxonomy. I leave it to you, dear reader, to sort it out. Send in your own binomials, Latin or otherwise, that best describe the various species, subspecies, and varieties of weavers you have observed. We'll publish the best and most useful of the lot in a future issue.

TIME *and* THREAD

"This was life as a great wheel."

I went to Bolivia to see a total eclipse of the sun and came back with visions and thoughts of time, and thread.

Time in Bolivia, as in other Third World countries, as in certain rare enclaves of our own, is not linear, does not have velocity. Watching an Indian family in a high mountain field putting in a crop—the man guiding a single-bladed plow pulled by a pair of oxen and a couple of children, the woman balancing a baby on her back while broadcasting seed grain from a handwoven bag—takes one right out of the present. There were no clues (except for our busload of passing tourists) that this was the twentieth century. This could have been 1860, or 1720, or 1590. This was life as a great wheel.

Thread in Bolivia is more tangled. There's a rich and varied tradition of excellent and interesting fabric such as is found throughout the Andes: intricate, imaginative, highly accomplished pick-up motifs woven, miraculously, on crude upright looms; knitted caps alive with pattern stranded in many colors at twelve or fourteen stitches to the inch; wildly colorful, complex sling braids produced offhandedly by small children; delicate knotted fringes that give a whole new meaning to the word macramé worked on handspun, handwoven alpaca mantas.

At the same time, there's a voracity for the new, the novel. Ancient, indigenous skills embrace whatever clever technique comes along. Every man and boy in every tiny, remote village seemed to have a handknitted sweater (often worn under a traditional woven poncho). Aran cables, Fair Isle X and O pattern bands, Scandinavian yoke sweaters with llamas instead of reindeer, masterfully executed and cleverly shaped to the wearer without the aid of printed instructions. Women on street corners selling newspapers were knitting complicated entrelac pullovers in cerise and magenta acrylic yarns; women tending curbside stalls of aromatic herbs and strange dried animal parts were knitting lacy cardigans of handspun natural-colored wool.

Dainty crocheted doilies of the finest white cotton. Colorful, cozy, spiral-knit caps on every ruddy-cheeked child. Those comical crocheted corkscrews that grandmas in this country attach to barrettes for their granddaughters' hair, which Indian women make in black to extend and adorn their long, shiny braids. Sturdy socks of handspun wool with curiously turned garter-stitch heels. All these and more, all made at top speed, at all times, without looking! Indian men improving on the backstrap loom by adopting Spanish-style two-shaft counterbalanced ones, but without a warp beam; instead, tying the end of the warp to a peg driven in the ground some distance away from the loom. Textiles offered for sale indiscriminately in the Indian markets, in the streets: exquisite but worn shawls, stiff and rank with dirt and age, held out side by side with equally well-made ponchos of indeterminate fiber content in screaming pink and chartreuse and royal blue.

My first reactions to these jarring incongruities were regret that the older techniques, the traditional hues and materials and styles aren't prevailing, and a tinge of condescension toward these people for preferring those hot, fake colors and trendy looks over the lovely old naturals and classic styles. But isn't that like saying that American weavers should all stick to blue-and-white overshot coverlets? That nobody should even think of doing triaxial weave with aluminized mylar and fishing line? (Well, maybe they shouldn't.)

I reread the chapter in Mary Meigs Atwater's *Weaving a Life* that describes her year's sojourn in Bolivia in 1906. In many ways, it could have been written today. True, the Indian women now have store-bought lace on their voluminous petticoats instead of hand-made needle lace, and minivans race through narrow streets meant only for foot traffic or the occasional burro carrying the same women with their shawls and little derby hats, the same shawls and hats you can see in an 88-year-old photograph in the book. So much has changed, yet so much endures.

In Praise *of* Thumbs

"I once taped mine to the palms of my hands for a day,

hoping maybe to experience a little regression or insight."

An oriole nest sits on a shelf in my office, a splendid, shimmering pouch made of nothing but horsehair and Christmas tree tinsel and couple of twigs. It came down in my backyard after a storm, this sturdy, airy, sparkling urn. There's no perceptible repeat pattern in its intricate interlacement, yet it's a uniformly well-made fabric. There's no telling what decision-making process (or its avian equivalent) was happening in some wee bird brain as its owner wove each filament in and out among the others. It is a miracle in every way. But the thought that crosses my mind every time I look at it is this: That bird had no hands!

Imagine making a complex textile using just your mouth. Granted, a bird beak is mechanically more like a human forefinger and thumb than a human mouth—but this nest is still astonishing. So forget your mouth, and imagine making something as simple as a three-strand braid with nothing but that pair of digits. You'll soon be grateful that you were designed with two hands and all those fingers. And as you fumble, you'll also give thanks that your thumb is made to pivot so cleverly.

Impressed by the assertion that our opposable thumbs were the first attribute to send humans on the evolutionary high road, I once taped mine to the palms of my hands for a day, hoping maybe to experience a little regression or insight. Frustration was more like it. So much of what most of us do in the course of a typical day— button a shirt, pick up a cup of coffee, tie a shoe—simply demands that offset thumb.

I remembered that old experiment recently while reading a novel in which one of the four characters was a pickpocket-turned-spy in Italy during World War II. In one grisly scene, his thumbs are amputated as punishment for some minor breach of identity, and he slides into a morphine-assisted depression that has far more to do with being thumbless than with being in pain.

The first bone of the thumb, the one that resides within the palm, is shorter and wider than those of the other fingers and set so that it faces inward. It is broad and flattened and concave, and designed for four complex muscle attachments that give the thumb its unusual strength and mobility. Although the thumb has only two phalanges as compared to three for the other fingers, its first has five muscle attachments, compared to two each for the other fingers. Its muscles extend deep into the forearm and intricately outward to the tip. A full description of the thumb's bones, ligaments, fascia, and muscles occupies volumes in the medical literature, and disorders of these parts provide lucrative careers for phalanxes (or phalanges) of hand surgeons. This is not just a short finger set cockeyed.

Even if you find yourself handicapped by arthritis or carpel tunnel syndrome, as so many of us who use our hands over a period of years do, those thumbs most likely play a key role when you weave. Imagine warping your loom without them. Possible, but no fun. As I type these words on my computer (using my index fingers to hit the space bar, just to see how that feels), it occurs to me that, sequencing problems aside, man could have evolved into a keyboard operator without thumbs, but not into a weaver of cloth. Two thumbs up for thumbs.

WORKING LIFE

"What's warp, what's weft?

What are the interlacements?"

I t's one of the oldest metaphors under the sun. The Bible used it, Shakespeare used it, Milton used it, the Chinese used it, Native Americans used it, a great many completely forgettable poets used it. It's too easy, really: The warp threads are the constants in your life, the major themes, and they go up and down. The weft picks are the variables—the triumphs, tragedies, tediums— that happen daily to make the fabric of your life. As weavers, we're especially drawn to the imagery.

I've had this on my mind lately because of being at that fulcrum, that midcentury mark that causes you to reexamine everything. My kids are scattered to the coasts, my parents have died. I'm writing this, in fact, as I sit in the middle of my late mother's living room in a quandary over all the boxes and heaps and piles that my brothers and I have to make decisions about. Here is her life scattered around me; there is mine, back in Colorado. What's warp, what's weft? What are the interlacements?

Things, with a capital T, were among the constants in my mother's life. Nobody needs as many pickle forks as this woman possessed, or cutwork linen napkins, or rubber bands, or string. She was not grasping or financially ambitious; it was just that Things were reliable amid the dozens of household moves and various personal losses and disappointments that shaped her life. Stockpiling, housekeeping, churchgoing, doing daily acts of kindness for whoever was at hand. These were her warp threads. Because she was a traditional woman of the sort who puts her needs and wants after everybody else's, her wefts were whatever circumstances brought her way.

If I had to characterize my mother's life as a kind of weaving, I would call it a rag rug—simple, strong warp, simple weave structures, and a make-do weft of other people's leavings. But it would lie flat, have good edges, withstand wear, and include bright, serendipitous color juxtapositions, because she was surprisingly complex in her own quiet, self-effacing way.

And what makes the fabric of my life? Work (I'm driven to making and building things), family (the kids are gone, but the bonds remain strong), I don't know what else; I'm not much given to this kind of introspection. I know my wefts are much more intentionally selected than my mother's were—it's easier for a woman to have choices now—and I expect my weave structure is a bit more intricate.

And how about yours? If you were to make a drawdown of your life and label each thread, what would be the constants, the warps? How long would your treadling sequence be? How predictable your pattern? Would you be a masterpiece of shaft switching, an even plaid, a lacy drift of deflected wefts? Does the actual cloth you choose to weave resemble the fabric of your life? Or your secret life?

It's no wonder weaving has been so overused as a metaphor for human existence—it just works. And we haven't even gotten into tie-ups, broken threads, dangling fringes, or supplementary warps. I can imagine a guild project made up of shared life-weaves that would rival those women's encounter groups of the seventies. I can imagine a sample book of all the people I'm close to. I can imagine this whole idea getting completely out of control.

STRINGING ALONG

"Yet here I am dealing in handmade futures."

I can't find the word "crastinate" in Webster's, but whatever its precise meaning, I'm in favor of it. You could call me a pro, in fact. I've crastinated actively and skillfully in almost everything I've ever undertaken: homework, housecleaning, weeding, writing my regular magazine columns, even spinning and weaving.

Regarding the last, though, I've found a way to turn my fault into a virtue. Or at least the illusion of a virtue. Or at least a way to keep people off my back. Here's how.

I love making things for friends and relatives. It's a special way of keeping people in mind, especially if I'm anxious about them. I remember long, long nights knitting a complicated cable sweater for my daughter when she was traveling in Eastern Europe and Africa, not available by phone for weeks on end. I'm sure those stitches kept her safe. I remember spending weekends weaving afghans and other useless items for my son when he went far away to school in a big city. He didn't get mugged (except once), and he graduated, so that's proof that my strategy worked. The reality is that, though people seem to enjoy receiving the things I make, the process probably means more to me than the object does to them.

I started applying my penchant for procrastination to my love of making gifts a few years ago. One of my coworkers was going to have a baby, and I wanted to spin and knit a little cap for it. By the time her shower came around, I had only got the spinning done. So I gave her the yarn with the understanding that she would return it to me and receive a finished cap soon. The "soon" ended up being when the baby was about three months old. The effect was that she got two gifts!

Another time, I spun several small batches of space-dyed silk top just for fun. As you may well know, there's not much you can do with randomly colored silk yarn that's not homely or at best surprising, so I gave each batch away with the promise that, if it were returned to me, it would find its way into a scarf for the donee. (That way I could put off having to figure out how to use it.) The most recent such magnanimous offering was made to a colleague in celebration of ten years of working together; eight months later, he's getting the scarf, with the silk as an accent yarn against a solid ground, and it looks okay. The gift that keeps giving (only not right away).

There are lots of ways to spin this process out even further. One year, I gave my son for his birthday a lovely black fleece, washed, carded, and dyed a dark charcoal green. For Christmas, he got a sweater's worth of yarn spun from the fleece. Next birthday, a sweater! Which didn't fit! By the time I had ripped out the bottom ribbing, lengthened it, put gussets under the arms, and gift-wrapped it yet again, it was time for another birthday. Four gifts from one project. It's the thought that counts.

I admit it's a racket, and I can't imagine why I'm sharing this personal nonsense with you. The fact is, I'm three baby caps and two silk scarves behind at this point and feeling a little panicked. I've never believed in buying things on layaway or running up my credit cards or going into debt. Yet here I am dealing in handmade gift futures.

An alternative, I suppose, would be to just give away the raw material and be done with it. I had a great-aunt who used to do that—give me yardage for Christmas. It shifted the burden of procrastination to me; I don't think I ever did get around to making anything out of those odd lots, but every time I looked in my sewing basket, I remembered her. I won't say how. Keep this in mind as we approach the holiday gift-making season.

pro · crast · in · ate *vb* [L *pro* forward; in favor of; *crassus gross,* thick; or *cras* tomorrow; L *ina,* fem. of *-inus,* of or belonging to; Gk *ate*: reckless or excessive folly that drives men to ruin]

1. To be in favor of waiting until tomorrow to engage in reckless folly that will result in a gross thing. 2. To be driven to ruin by getting in the thick of things.

—from the Ligon Lexicon

I LOVE

MY COMPUTER

"Actually, the computer would rather

I didn't talk about heddles at all; it would be happier

with hectic, hector, hedonist, or hee-haw."

Computers are amazing. I use one in the same way that, say, a caveman might have used a Cuisinart. I see what it does, but I don't really have a clue how (or sometimes why). Take its word-processing capability. I spent countless hours in elementary school drilling on rules of punctuation, grammar, and spelling, and I take great pride in my mastery of these language elements.

So here I sit at my handy laptop (I can plug it in anywhere: the car, the vacation cabin, the boudoir, the bathroom), converting thoughts into words on a screen. My computer is pleased to tell me that 1) the sentence you are just now reading is passive (WRONG!), 2) this paragraph has a 70.7 percent readability index, 3) I should say cavedweller, not caveman, and 4) I'm writing at about a seventh-grade level. This is worse than having my grade school English teacher, Miss Lillard, sitting on my shoulder for life.

As a weaving tool, the computer is something else again. It's often been said that the loom was the first computer. This makes good cocktail party talk, unless you socialize with engineering types, in which case you will get wary looks. ("Yeah, right, lady," these young whippersnappers are thinking, "like a broom was the first telephone.") Or worse, they might ask you to explain what you mean.

The fact is, though, that looms and computers have become quite intimately linked. You can buy computer software that will give you that warm, fuzzy weaving experience without ever having to touch thread. You can "warp" your "loom" and "weave" your "cloth" a jillion different ways with just a few keystrokes, and no danger of ending up with some ugly thing that no one would want (or of having to crawl under a big piece of furniture with a bunch of dustballs and tie knots).

If weaving virtual fabric on a computer is a little too airy for your taste, you can weave on a real loom with your computer. That is, you can hook your computer right up to your loom, plug the whole mess in, and just sit there stomping on a couple of treadles while the computer does all the fun parts, like deciding which shafts to lift so that you get a nice pattern. Of course, you still have to put all those threads through all those little holes and stomp and fling the shuttle back and forth. It's sort of like doing the plain background in needlepoint, only more athletic. It's also sort of like the Sorcerer's Apprentice.

Finally, you can use a computer to write about weaving. Problem is, unless you have taken the time to train it, you can be pretty sure that your computer doesn't know squat about the subject. If you try to use its wonderful advanced features, such as the spelling checker or thesaurus, you might be in for some rude surprises. Take a sentence like this: "Sley the warp at twelve ends per inch in a six-dent reed after threading each end through the appropriate heddle." Makes perfect sense, doesn't it? Until the computer gets hold of it. Right away, it's going to want to change "sley" to "sleepy." I understand this because there's nothing that makes me want to take a nap more than sleying a reed unless it's threading a heddle (oops, make that meddle, or . . . hedge). Actually, the computer would rather I didn't talk about heddles at all; it would be happier with hectic, hector, hedonist, or hee-haw. As in, "Get in there and thread your hee-haw, woman!" I also understand why the computer would gladly change "reed" to "redundancy."

After you've dressed your loom (for which you perhaps employed a rackety, racy, radiant, radical raddle), then there's the challenge of actually weaving cloth. And you can't write about weaving cloth without writing about that pesky weft. Does it surprise you that my computer doesn't recognize the word "weft," and so wants to change it to "weep," or even "weep loudly"? I thought not.

OH, WHAT A TANGLED WEB WE WEAVED

"What did I do on Sunday afternoon?

I weaved.

Where did I get that funky scarf?

I weaved it myself."

It's hard to recover from being an English teacher. I was one for a while about twenty-five years ago, and I still become livid over such nonsense as "it's" as a possessive. As in "A place for everything and everything in it's place." Having everything in its place is not the issue, as you would quickly perceive if you saw my desk, my yarn shelves, or my sock drawer (where I recently found my nametag from last year's Northern California Weavers' Conference and a few of my twenty-one-year-old son's baby teeth). It's just that old-teacher pickiness; it's hard to shed.

Ill-formed possessives, disagreement between nouns and pronouns, writing "like" when you mean "as"—odious! Yet there's one contrarian usage that I am devoted to. I prefer to say that I weaved instead of I wove. What did I do on Sunday afternoon? I weaved. Where did I get that funky scarf? I weaved it myself. It's an embarrassing eccentricity, yet I can't quite give it up.

Maybe it has to do with the poverty of past tenses in the English language: I wove, I have or had woven. That's about all you get. Compare that with some of the American Indian languages that have six, nine, fourteen or more ways of expressing degrees of pastness— earlier today, yesterday, a fortnight ago, so long ago no one can quite remember when, in the days of the ancestors, and so on. How rich and precise! You can choose to be absolutely done with something, or select some degree of ongoing connection. Even if I haven't picked up a shuttle in a month, I like to think that I am continually a weaver (even if a lax one), and "weaved," as opposed to "wove," somehow implies that continuity. Furthermore, "wove" sounds mournful.

So imagine how pleased I was to read syndicated columnist James Kilpatrick address this very subject in the Sunday paper a few weeks ago. A reader had queried whether it was better to say that a rugmaker weaved a rug or wove a rug? Kilpatrick's judicious reply didn't quite answer my need, but it went a long way. "The court," he said, "will declare that it all depends. It is a matter of sound, cadence, and context. The writer's ear must choose between a long 'o' or a long 'e', between one syllable or two, and the writer must make judgment calls. The court," he continued, "believes a speeding driver weaved his way through traffic, but the overture wove a spell."

Given that latitude, I'll take weaved every time. And furthermore, when my husband asks me what I did all evening, you can be sure I'll tell him I spinned, not spun.

RAVELINGS

"It would be easy to say that,

in the grand scheme of things,

our fiber craft wasn't very important.

But it was important."

During the early years of my marriage, before I began spinning and weaving, before I started Interweave Press, there were a few years that I stayed home with my babies and tried to be a good corporate wife. I belonged to a lot of different organizations, put in huge amounts of volunteer time.

There was my church, the Unitarian Church, where almost everyone had the same values and lots of the same interests, read the same books, drove the same Volvos, signed the same petitions, supported the same causes.

There were political groups, including the party that I served as precinct captain, in which everybody tended to think the same thoughts, support the same candidates, share the same ideologies, slap on the same bumper stickers.

There was the Great Books program, where we all read the same stuff and mostly agreed on what it meant. There was PTA, where everybody was more or less the same age, lived in the same neighborhood, had kids the same age with the same childhood diseases at the same time. And so on.

In each of these groups I felt that some part of me—the political part, the spiritual part, the mommy part—fit right in. But it wasn't until I began to spin and weave and found my local spinners' and weavers' guild, a hodgepodge of ages, backgrounds, lifestyles, skill levels, and tastes, all tied together with a tenuous thread of interest in an unusual and somewhat obsolete pursuit, that I felt the whole me was completely at home, completely accepted.

The only thing the members of my guild had in common was

a love of fiber and a love of potlucks. And for sure, none of us ever spun or wove the same thing, not even close! There were traditional weavers of traditional coverlets done the right way, there were weavers of gaudy fringed clothing (this was the '70s), there were old hippies and middle-aged country club matrons and grandmas and even a few grandpas, professional women, university students, full-time moms, you name it. We came together once a month and simply felt at home with each other.

The things we talked about—how to improve our selvedges, how to scour a particularly nasty fleece, where to find the neatest new yarns, how to salvage a disaster, what new craft book to read— were worlds apart from politics, social problems, child-rearing challenges, natural disasters, and other weighty matters. It would have been easy to say that, in the grand scheme of things, our fiber craft wasn't very important. But it was important. It was the ballast, the glue, the center, for the intricate balancing acts we were all doing with the rest of our lives.

It was important because weaving and spinning have been part of human culture from time before time, a truly important part of our evolution as a species. Our crafts have been an expression of human ingenuity, of the human capacity to develop an aesthetic sense, of the human attribute of opposable thumbs. Because fiber crafts are slow, labor intensive, time intensive, they have forever been behaviors that allow and encourage their practitioners to slow down, stop, pay attention, get beneath the surface of the demands of daily life, exercise care, create beauty.

These pursuits are antidotes to haste, impatience, pressure, conformity. They remind us to respect the natural world and the materials it provides. They give us a sense of continuity with our past, and a sense of linkage with other cultures. They connect us with weavers and spinners from other times, other places. When you practice these crafts, you end up with so much more than a bunch of placemats or a jacket or a nice wall hanging. You end up with new reverberations in your life—how you look at things, what you value.

You can be a weaver or a spinner all by yourself. But if you're lucky enough to belong to a guild, you can do it with other kindred spirits—friends who understand that these crafts have to do with much more than interlacing or looping or stitching or throwing a shuttle.

YARN

CONFESSIONS

"The real question that emerged was,

Why do I have all this yarn?"

W
hile we were away visiting our son and daughter-in-law last spring, our basement flooded, and I didn't discover the soggy, unfortunate fact for almost a week. In terms of bother, it meant picking up every single thing and moving it so the carpet could be ripped out. In terms of loss, it meant throwing out all the paperback novels on the bottom shelf of the bookcase (their bottom edges were stuck together and turning green) and all the grade-school papers that had accumulated between 1971and 1986 that nobody would ever look at again anyhow. Also some bottom-shelf yarn, but not much. It could have been a lot worse.

When finally, with moldy heaps removed and new carpet in place, I set about reorganizing everything—first and foremost of which were my yarn shelves—I was faced with the opportunity to create a new order, and the quandary of deciding what it should be.

Here's how the yarn was before: All naturals grouped together (whites, grays, browns, blacks) regardless of fiber, unless they were linen. All dyed colors grouped by color family regardless of fiber (unless they were linen, or very shiny, or very skinny, or very precious). All embroidery floss in one basket, regardless of color (because it was very skinny). All linen together, regardless of color (because it was very skinny and because it was linen). In other words, my own system, if you could call it that. But clearly, it could be improved on, and this was the opportune time.

How about a continuum from the prettiest yarn to the ugliest? With the ugly on the bottom shelf so it would get the kabosh next time the basement flooded. Or how about yarn I'm likely to need or want to use versus yarn that will never, ever have any use whatsoever (sort of like those old grade-school papers)? Or maybe by imaginary project. Some of my yarn was actually bought with a purpose in mind, but most of it would require some creative shuffling to be woven into something presentable and come out even. Or I could arrange it chronologically, with all the 1970s putrid green and gold on one side, segueing to the 1990s wines and purples on the other. Would organizing it this way increase the odds of its getting used? Not likely. The real question that emerged was, Why do I have all this yarn?

The fact is, I'm a hoarder. Having the yarn is something of an end in itself. When I feel the urge to weave, I survey my hoard and, more often than not, go out and buy more. More than sixty percent of the readers of this magazine have confessed, when scientifically surveyed, to the same habit. Why is this? I'm reminded of an elderly neighbor from many years ago who had been through the Great Depression and had taken it hard. She had a basement filled with shelves and freezers of food. Store-bought canned food, homemade canned food, month-old bread, grocery store bargains of every description. Here's how extreme she was: she would buy big bags of cornmeal on sale. When they got weevily (which they inevitably did), she would cook up huge disgusting batches of weevily cornbread and feed it to her chickens (secret chickens which she shouldn't legally have had in town).

I have yarn that's the equivalent of that weevily cornmeal. I've actually contemplated weaving it up into whatever and giving it away to strangers. Why didn't I just pitch it when I was cleaning the basement? You tell me.

WEAVING
HONOR ROLL

"Shouldn't it be written somewhere

that these people were the mainstays of the craft?

That they taught and inspired

an exponential number of others?"

When I heard that Everett Gilmore had passed away recently, in his sleep at the admirable age of almost ninety-eight, one of the first things I did was go back into my correspondence files. Mr. Gilmore, maker of fine looms for more than sixty years, was also a prolific letter writer. Over the years, I had heard from him at great length about the various improvements he was experimenting with in his loom factory, goings-on of his cousins, nieces, and nephews, weaving projects he was undertaking (rag rugs for his mobile home! Curtains for his whole house!), the state of health of his little dog. Tucked in amongst almost twenty years' worth of communication was a letter he had received from Mary Meigs Atwater back in the 1940s and passed on to me as a curiosity. Much the same sort of chat: looms, weaving, travels, the weather.

It occurred to me as I read through the file that I don't know very many people who actually knew Mary Atwater well. And how long will it be before there won't be many of us around who knew Everett Gilmore? Who, I wondered, is keeping track?

Since I started weaving in the early 1970s, so many fine weavers, influential teachers, prolific writers about weaving and spinning, and just simply dear people have left us. For me, there's Louise Green, Norma Walker, Edna Blackburn, Ednah Illsley, Art Ronin, Laya Brostoff, Walt Schutz, Anne Blinks, Beverly Royce—the list could go on and on. And I'll bet that most everyone reading this has a list. Shouldn't it be written somewhere that these people were mainstays of the craft? That they taught and inspired an exponential number of others? We publish short obituaries in the magazine as we hear about these losses, but mightn't there be a better organized, more intentional effort to remember?

Well, there could, and it would be simple. If you, every one of you, would write a single page about each of the weavers and spinners you have known who deserves a place in our collective memory for having taught, encouraged, helped, created, or otherwise exemplified good craftsmanship and good sharing, and if you would send that page or those pages here to Interweave, we could compile a memory book, an honor roll, that would stand as a living record. We could publish all or part of the names on the list from time to time as a reminder.

Here's what I'd like to invite you to do. Write such a sheet, a single sheet, for as many departed craftsmen or -women as you please. You can use typewriter, word processor, or old-fashioned handwriting (neatly legible, of course). Head the sheet with the person's name, dates of birth and death (if you know them), and home town. Then write informally and briefly about their weaving life. Did they belong to a guild? Did they teach? What kind of work did they do? Did they achieve any recognition for it? Did they make looms? Sell yarn? What sets them apart in memory? Personal traits? Funny stories? You get the idea. And please enclose a picture if you have one.

Don't fold your pages up! Keep them neatly flat, put them in a big envelope, and send them here to Interweave Press, c/o Weaving

Honor Roll. Tell your friends. If you'll do your part, we'll do ours of keeping this record organized and safe. It's another way of weaving, another kind of yarn.

A Loom-shaped Life

"There's ingenuity inherent in loom-shaping,

a combination of preplanning and spontaneity,

suppleness, and flexibility."

I was working on a beadweaving project recently for our new magazine, *Interweave Beadwork*, and found myself employing an old weaver's trick, warp pulling. That is, to weave a neckpiece that curved nicely, I just left deep wedge-shaped segments of the warp unwoven, and then when the piece was finished, pulled on the warps to snug those areas together into neat curves. You've probably tried this at one time or another—to create invisible darts in a garment, for instance. Kerry Evans took the idea to the limit in a good little book a few years ago—a whole wardrobe of shapely garments that depend entirely on pulled warps rather than seams and darts for their shape and fit.

Even more basic: almost every weaver in the world has woven a bog jacket or one of its relatives at one time or another. Figuring out how to shape a piece of fabric on the loom so that, voila, with a minimum number of folds and seams it's transformed into something great to wear—something that has places to stick your arms, room for your bosom, something that actually fits yet doesn't look anything at all as though it came out of the Simplicity pattern book—has been the basis of whole books, whole weaving careers.

Fabric, in its malleability, is sculptural; garments are body-shaped soft sculptures; bodies are not, as a rule, precisely tubular. Yet as loom weavers we work within a decisively rectangular grid that wants to produce right angles and tubes. Defying that grid is one of the perpetual challenges of weaving. The easy out, of course, is just taking a pair of scissors to the finished cloth and cutting the shapes we need. We find all kinds of reasons not to do that, though—fear of cutting, abhorrence of waste. After all, having personally handled every warp and every weft and overseen every intersection of the two, we have a keener sense of the value (and vulnerability) of the fabric than your average seamstress.

So we do tricks to shape the fabric on the loom such as pulling warps or weaving jogs and slits that will fit together cleverly when we're done. No matter how sophisticated our looms become or how smart the sewing machines and interlock-overcasting devices that make cutting and seaming safe and easy, many of us still take up the challenge of beating the grid. It's either a mental challenge or a point of honor, or sometimes both.

I thought about this all the time I was making my beaded neck-piece (which was quite a while, believe me, counting out thirty beads in proper color sequence for each and every row) and "loom-shaped" became a sort of mantra that led to contemplation of the loom-shaped life. I got to thinking about how my life might have been different if I hadn't had that loom in the corner of my living room for the past twenty-five years, hadn't been weaving cloth in my head as a handy distraction in two decades of slow meetings or nights of insomnia, hadn't analyzed every stranger's sport coat fabric, hadn't pondered how to weave every striking sunset or cross section of geological strata that came down the road, hadn't had weaving friends to hang out with who understood me perfectly because they're weavers, too. What would I have been thinking? Doing? This is idle speculation, of course. Like what if I hadn't had that first date with my husband, or conceived a particular child, or gotten sick before a critical job interview. If my life hadn't been loom-shaped, it would have been shaped by something else, no doubt. Still, I like the idea of a loom-shaped life.

Loom-shaping a woven piece means transcending the limitations of a grid while working within it. Pulling warps to shape a woven piece means accepting the limits of a warp while rejecting the convention that warp ends have to be the same length. There's ingenuity inherent in loom-shaping, a combination of preplanning and spontaneity, suppleness and flexibility. We're lucky to be weavers— there's so much to learn.

GO, DOG, GO

"It became what we in the weaving world

have come to call 'a dog on the loom.'"

Sometimes you put a long warp on your loom when you only need a short one, because it's no more work. Right? And sometimes, after you've woven off the amount you really needed, that extra warp sits there and haunts you. If you're such a precise and disciplined weaver that you can't relate to what I've just said, turn the page, because you're not going to have much patience with what follows.

I put a 10/2s cotton warp on my loom several months ago to weave some towels for a hostess gift and a housewarming gift. Two pairs of small towels. Four yards plus loom waste was all I needed. So why did I put on ten yards?

Because I had a really huge cone of yarn. Because it was no more work to put on a long warp than a short one. Because I would then have all that "free" warp to play around with, to weave extras with, to get ahead of the game with. What I didn't reckon on was how little I would enjoy weaving that particular warp. There wasn't anything really wrong with it, except that the color was a bit morose, the treadling tedious.

I did get the four towels done—they looked just fine, they were functional—but having fulfilled my immediate gift needs, I just couldn't go back and finish that warp. It was too good to abandon, not good enough to claim my time. So the remaining six or so yards of warp have been sitting there gathering dust ever since, transforming my good old loom into a moping hulk in the corner of my living room. I just couldn't make myself cut it off and cut my losses. It became what we in the weaving world have come to call a "dog on the loom."* Perhaps you've had one yourself. Perhaps you have one right now.

This past weekend I had a breakthrough, and I'd like to share it with you, because it could herald a small handweaving revival in this country. Let's say there are 100,000 active weavers in America (an unprovable number our market research keeps coming up with). Let's say ten percent of them have a warp blockage, a "dog" on their loom. I think that's a conservative estimate. That means there are 10,000 looms taking up space in the living rooms of America clogged with reject warps, preventing their owners from getting on with what they really love to do.

Okay. Now imagine that there are 10,000 nice people out there who would love to try their hand at weaving if someone would just point them in the right direction. I'm positive that there are that many and more. You see where I'm headed with this? If you have a dog on your loom, invite your nonweaving friend over, show her or him how to press the treadles and throw the shuttle. This will take about ten minutes. Then you can go bake muffins or something while your objectionable warp goes away. Your friend will be thrilled, you will have enlarged the community of weaving enthusiasts, and you can get busy planning your next project.

This does work. Just ask my son's girlfriend.

* The term "dog on the loom" was coined by Debbie Allen lots of years ago in an essay in *Handwoven* magazine.

How I Became

an

Ugly American

"It's a treasure, it's an albatross.

I have it, but it's not mine."

I saw it in a tourist shop in Mexico, flung on a shelf amid the usual stuff: bright pottery, Aztec gods, naughty little clay figures, painted wooden jaguars. ¿Cuanto cuesta? I asked in my pathetic high-school Spanish. Not for sale, the shop girl answered, in comparable English.

I couldn't let it go, though. The sturdy, golden brown two-ply yarn, probably henequen, almost surely thigh-spun, perfect. The seamless, flawless, netted construction, perfect. The elegant, stout, twined border, dyed with cochineal but faded to a lovely shell pink. I'd never seen such a beautiful bag, and I wanted it.

I stopped in again the next day, and asked was she sure she didn't want to sell it? After many gestures, she made me understand that she'd have to ask the owner. At first I thought she meant the owner of the shop, and I supposed the bag was a special display piece, because it was by far the finest thing to be seen. But it soon became clear that it was the owner of the bag she needed to confer with—a shabby looking man hanging out in the back. Two hundred pesos, he said. I could hardly believe my luck! Twenty-five dollars for the most beautiful bag in the world! Sí, I'll take it! I didn't even try to bargain.

It is old, I understood him to say—maybe forty or fifty years old. It comes from Chiapas. They don't make them anymore like this. I gestured all kinds of enthusiastic appreciation, and started counting out my pesos. He pocketed them, and began to remove his personal odds and ends from the bag. And as he handed it to me, he reverently kissed it goodbye.

Can you imagine what I felt? He was selling me something precious, something made perhaps by his grandmother. I wanted to say keep it! Keep the money, too!—because he clearly needed it. All kinds of schemes ran through my brain—return the bag, slip the money in his pocket. Leave the bag on the street where he might find it. Give him all the money in my purse on some wild pretext. But in fact, he had struck a deal, his pride in the value of this possession was clear, he wore his Mayan macho pride like a mantle.

So this wonderful henequen bag is mine. I carry it to work every day. I ponder on its venerable sweat stains, admire the natural crease on the bottom where the netting changes direction, marvel at the inscrutable way in which the netting joins the twined edge. It's a treasure, it's an albatross. I have it, but it's not mine.

KIDS' WEAVING

"What we really hope is that there will be somebody

we can leave our looms to."

I have babies on my mind. This afternoon, my one and only grandchild, Ben, will be coming for a week's visit. He's flying here from Boston with my husband (who went to fetch him, since he's only two years old). I've spent the weekend digging out old children's books, rallying matchbox trucks, moving glassware strategically, and making sure we have plenty of Cheerios. In the back of my mind, I've been reviewing a remarkable exhibit I saw last week at Convergence 98 in Atlanta.

It was a great concept: weaving done by children with the mentoring of members of the Handweavers' Guild of America. Much of the work happened in classrooms, notably the first-grade classroom of Geri Forkner, a teacher in Decatur, Georgia. Geri cleverly put a looong multicolored warp on a small floor loom (I'm guessing) and encouraged the children to weave it off mostly with carpet warp in plain weave, but with accent stripes of whatever they pleased. Whatever they pleased! Given permission, it's amazing what children will please. Ribbons, rags, paper, strings of paper clips, button bands, tinsel, you name it. The work was lively, engaging, individual, exhuberant. And the selvedges weren't too bad, either.

Elsewhere in the exhibit was a group of pieces that made me look twice—a set of simple placemats, maybe 10/2 cotton, woven by, or with the help of, so help me, a two-year-old. Now, I'm trying to imagine my Ben weaving placemats. "Here, Ben, put this shuttle through this little space while Nana holds the treadle down. Oops, no, Ben, don't run out the door with it! Oh, you'd rather play trucks with the nice shuttle? You want to see if the pretty thread will stretch all the way out to the mailbox?" I could probably get Ben to weave a few picks if I duct-taped him to the loom bench and firmly guided his little hands, but I think his mama would object.

During my kids' toddler years, weaving happened at our house mostly during their nap times—maybe I was underestimating them. (Or maybe I knew my own limits.) They didn't really start coming into their own weaving-wise until they were six or seven. And they each had their own style. Ethan wanted to finish his first project in a hurry, and after that it was "been there, done that." Liz liked fancy twills and making gifts—scarves, ponchos—for friends and teachers. Day was by far the most dextrous and speedy, and had the greatest attention span. He tried tapestry, but really loved to bang out cloth fast on a little floor loom. He designed and wove a table runner when he was in second grade, and amazed me with his persistence and efficiency.

We in the weaving community often speak of passing the craft on to the next generation. We hope that kids who are exposed to traditional crafts will not only appreciate them more, but will someday, when they're grown, remember how much fun it all was and pick it up again. What we really hope is that there will be somebody we can leave our looms to. It's hard for me to visualize any of my kids—the economist, the lawyer, the herpatologist— ever weaving again. So maybe it will skip a generation. Maybe I'd better get out the duct tape.

WHEN I AM
AN OLD WOMAN

"Will I really become

a patient, deliberate weaver some day?"

Well, I probably will wear purple, because I've always worn purple. On the other hand, I probably won't spit or sit in the middle of sidewalks or do most of the other forms of acting out listed in the poem that we've all come to know so well.* What's in question is whether or not I'll get around to tackling any of the myriad projects I've always imagined myself doing "when I'm an old woman."

Learning fine bookbinding. Taking up the cello. Mastering Spanish. Organizing the family snapshots. Or, for heaven's sake, using up all that yarn. This last ambition is probably the least likely to be achieved because some of the yarn is upwards of twenty-five years old and is now really, really ugly. I look at it and try to imagine if there's anyone in the world I could give it to without incurring bad karma.

More likely to be realized, and more fun to contemplate, is my secret weaving ambition. It's been lying dormant for many years— ever since Thomas and the kids and I built our little mountain cabin back in the 1980s. The cabin is remote and primitive—that is, no electricity, phone, or indoor plumbing—but it's light and cozy and very, very quiet. My idea has been to someday do a whole different kind of weaving at our cabin from what I do, or have done, at home.

At home, I've got my shelves and shelves of yarn (it's not all ugly), my trusty jack loom, my electric bobbin winder, all the conveniences. At the cabin, I've got acres of raw material and presumably, someday, all the time in the world. I, who generally buy my yarn ready-made by the skein and cone, imagine spinning fleece and dyeing golds and greens and tans and violets with all the plants and lichens on our little mountain patch. I, who cherish my shafts and treadles and foot-powered sheds and end-delivery shuttles, and who love to bang out yardage as fast as possible, imagine making my own Navajo-style loom from native timbers and weaving tapestries slowly, pick by pick. I imagine my lovely yarns piled in a basket I've made of the red-twig dogwood that grows along our stream, and my tapestries glowing softly on our pine log walls.

What do you think? Will it happen? Will I really become a patient, deliberate weaver some day, or will I just tromp around our acres and then loll about the cabin reading murder mysteries, as I do now? Do you have fantasies of this sort, of becoming a different kind of person when you're old? Of developing patience if you've always been hasty, or daring if you've always been careful? Do you actually know anyone who's made such a change of style and temperament, unless he or she has become demented? I don't, but that doesn't mean it can't be done.

The real question is this: How will I know when I've gotten to be an old woman?

*The poem, "When I am an old woman I shall wear purple," by Anon, appears in a collection of the same name edited by Sandra Haldeman Martz and published in 1991 by Papier Mache Press.

WEFT CROSSING WARP

"The natural cycles and self-corrections even things out

and life goes on, it would seem, unchanged."

The other day I noticed a ghost from the past hanging on the coat rack here at Interweave Press. It was a handwoven "bog" coat of brushed wool in soft earthy stripes, and it appeared as a project in the very first issue of *Handwoven* twenty years ago. Sometimes on a chilly day, someone will slip it on while she goes about her data entry or phone calling or whatever. I doubt that any of the sixty-five or so people who work here knows that this garment has a history, since only a couple of them have been here all this time. It's just part of the landscape, handy to throw on when the furnace isn't cranking.

Seeing that rather forlorn coat got me to thinking about how much has changed here over the last twenty years. The woman who designed and wove the coat—where is she now? What about the other weavers who contributed to that first issue? You'll find a few of them in these pages, but there are so many more who have gone on to other pursuits, dropped out of sight, passed away. And whatever happened to bog coats, anyway? And all that fringe? Yet the weaving continues. It looks different in some regards, but it's still essentially weft crossing warp, just as weaving has been for at least 4,000 years.

I've been reading a marvelous book, *The Beak of the Finch* by Jonathan Weiner. It's the story of a couple of biologists who have been studying Darwin's finches in the Galápagos for the past twenty years. What they've found is that evolution happens daily, seasonally, annually among these bird populations. One year skinny-beaked birds will thrive because of the kind of seed most available, and reproduce their kind. Another year, those skinny-beaked birds won't be able to crack the big hard seeds that are most abundant, so they decline in numbers. Some years the changes are profound—85 percent mortality, followed by a straggly new generation with a new mix of distinguishing traits. Yet if you take the long view, comparing the birds of twenty years ago with the birds of today, the changes are virtually imperceptible. The natural cycles and self-corrections even things out and life goes on, it would seem, unchanged.

Over the years, this magazine has had a fairly stable population of between 20,000 and 24,000 subscribers (with another 10,000 or so who pick it up here and there). Yet every year, 4,000 or 5,000 don't renew their subscription, for one reason or another. And 4,000 or 5,000 brand new readers take their place. Isn't that interesting? Can't you just imagine Darwin peering at us, taking notes?

ON THE EDGE

"The edges are lively, challenging, dangerous,

fraught with spiders."

Here's what I saw on the bike path a couple of weeks ago: In the stubbly grass right alongside the paving, trap-door spiders had built webs every eighteen inches for more than a mile. It was astonishing! The early morning sun caught the dew in their shallow saucer-sized funnels; it was a mile-long glittering, wispy necklace of spiderly mischief.

Why did they choose this very public thoroughfare instead of scattering themselves through the adjoining prairie? Because there's more action, more opportunity for breakfast there on the margin.

I've noticed that kind of life along the edge other times, too. Walking our rural road at night alongside a cornfield, I've heard the scurry of a field mouse every twelve paces, clockwork predictable. The mice stake out their frontage as cannily as fast-food restaurants along a freeway. It's not just my fantasy; Terry Tempest Williams has written knowingly and deeply of life on the edge in *An Unspoken Hunger: Stories from the Field.*

So what does this have to do with weaving? It's about those edges. Those edges that we take pride in, or despair of, or flaunt, or apologize for, or try to hide. Those edges that are sometimes said to be the mark of weaving skill.

Think about this: The middle of a piece of loom-woven cloth, unless it involves tapestry or inlay, pretty much takes care of itself. Thread and sley and wind on with precision, and you hardly have to give it another thought. Throw the shuttle, cloth is made. But the edges—they demand constant vigilance. The edges are where tension is likely to go awry; where draw-in is almost inevitable, progressing gradually until you're suddenly ambushed with frayed or snapped warp threads or a bunched-up fell. The edges are lively, challenging, dangerous, fraught with spiders. Just think how many hints and tips in your average weaving book or magazine are devoted to managing the edges. The sage advice tends to fall into categories:

1. Fight with tooth and nail—not to mention fishing weights, rheostats, C-clamps, and spiky temples—for smooth edges. Force those edges to be civilized.

2. Defeat them with pickiness. Lay every weft in with dainty care, adjusting and pinching and patting every turn to perfection. (Finish one piece of cloth every five years.)

3. Let your loom do the work. Use floating selvedges that can bear a great deal of tension so they won't draw in, or use a couple of extra shafts just for the edges. Sounds easy, but the loom doesn't really do the work—it takes a lot of technique.

4. Hide them. Conceal them in seams or bindings or cut them off!

5. Flaunt their imperfection. Ripply edges? Hey, it's handwoven!

6. My favorite: make them the design focus of your weaving. If you're going to have to fuss around and be anxious about your edges, make them worth the bother.

For instance: Weave a fairly plain fabric, but put fancy patterned stripes along each edge. The very first pashmina shawls I saw in New York—before absolutely everybody was selling or wearing those lovely clichés—were solid natural gray cashmere with dainty, elegant, narrow silk patterned borders with a touch of embroidery.

(What was smart about that was the silk was strong and could take a higher tension.) You often see the same idea on Indian sari fabrics.

Weave a fairly plain fabric, and embellish the edges afterward. Charlotte Allison, of Long Branch, Texas, sews a tiny seed bead on every edge loop of her lovely scarves—a quiet celebration of very good (but not totally perfect) selvedges. Or weave a fabric but weave extraordinary edges of a different structure while you're at it. Great examples: card-woven selvedges on weft-faced rugs, à la Martha Stanley. Or intricate tubular braids on textiles of the Andean Highlands (for which see *Bolivian Tubular Edging & Andean Crossed-Warp Technique* by Adele Cahlendar, Dos Tejedoras/Interweave Press).

What you do with your edges will depend on your nature (patient or not, assertive or shy), your attention span (fiddle with them or let 'em rip), or any number of other variables. Next time you sit at your loom, though, think about those trap-door spiders (those arachnids to whom we are related in legend and folklore), weaving and unweaving and weaving and unweaving their cunning little webs, and finding all the bugs they need along the verge.

ALL ESSAYS WERE ORIGINALLY PRINTED IN *HANDWOVEN* MAGAZINE
A PUBLICATION OF INTERWEAVE PRESS